POPULAR SONGS

HAL LEONARD
TUDENT PIANO LIBRARY

Double Agent!
Piano

Eight Arrangements for One Piano, Four Hands

Arranged by Jeremy Siskind

ISBN 978-1-4803-5280-3

HAL•LEONARD®
CORPORATION

7777 W. BLUEMOUND RD. P.O.BOX 13819 MILWAUKEE, WI 53213

Visit Hal Leonard Online at
www.halleonard.com

Introduction

Secrecy, deception, beautiful heroines, high stakes, fast chases, futuristic gadgets, treacherous villains, and suave style: spy movies have all the best elements of a summer blockbuster. Over the century that spy films have been giving audiences thrills and chills, their theme music has been just as electrifying as the on-screen action. The spy themes in this collection are among the most recognizable melodies in popular music and can be heard in video games, at sports matches, and in commercials. They range from the surf-rock coolness of the "James Bond Theme" to the sly swing of "The Pink Panther," from the exhilarating urgency of the "Mission: Impossible Theme" to the funky grooves of "Soul Bossa Nova" from the *Austin Powers* franchise.

Being a secret agent is all about knowing whom you can and can't trust. Playing piano duets is no different! It takes trust, patience, and sensitivity to be a good duet partner. Make sure to find a partner who listens well, who plays with sensitivity, and who will dedicate as much practice time to these pieces as you will. You should also be 100% sure that your partner isn't selling secrets to your nemesis.

So, find a reliable sidekick, make sure you're not bugged, have an escape route planned, and enjoy playing the music in *Double Agent!*

–Jeremy Siskind

Contents

Get Smart
from the Television Series

By Irving Szathmary
Arranged by Jeremy Siskind

Inspector Clouseau Theme

By Henry Mancini
Arranged by Jeremy Siskind

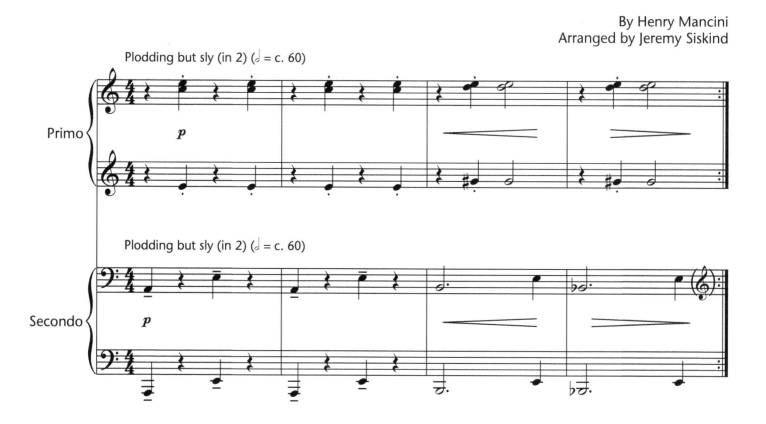

11

Inspector Gadget
(Main Title)
Theme from the TV Cartoon INSPECTOR GADGET

Words and Music by Haim Saban
and Shuki Levy
Arranged by Jeremy Siskind

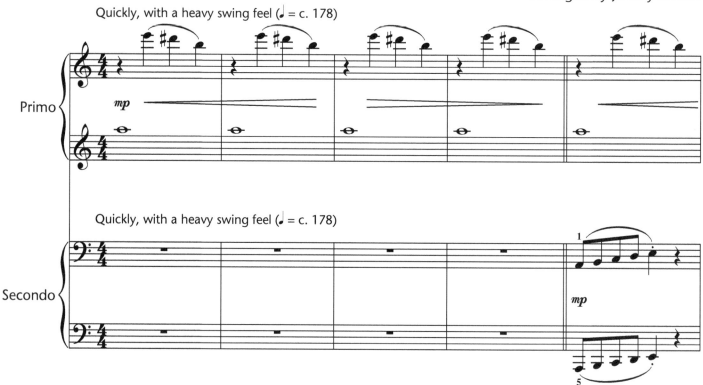

18

James Bond Theme

By Monty Norman
Arranged by Jeremy Siskind

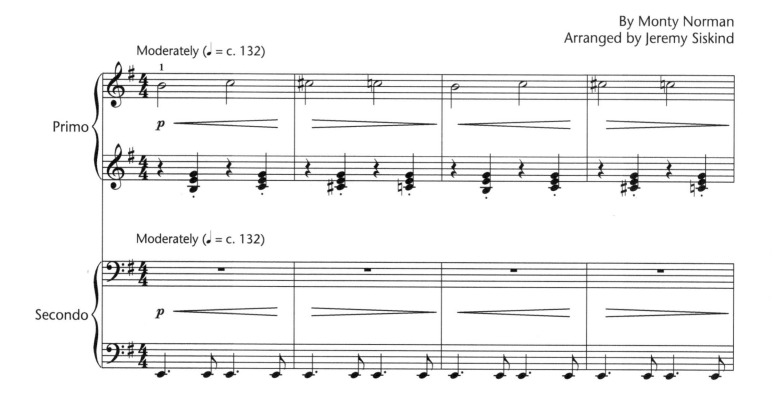

Mission: Impossible Theme

from the Paramount Television Series MISSION: IMPOSSIBLE

By Lalo Schifrin
Arranged by Jeremy Siskind

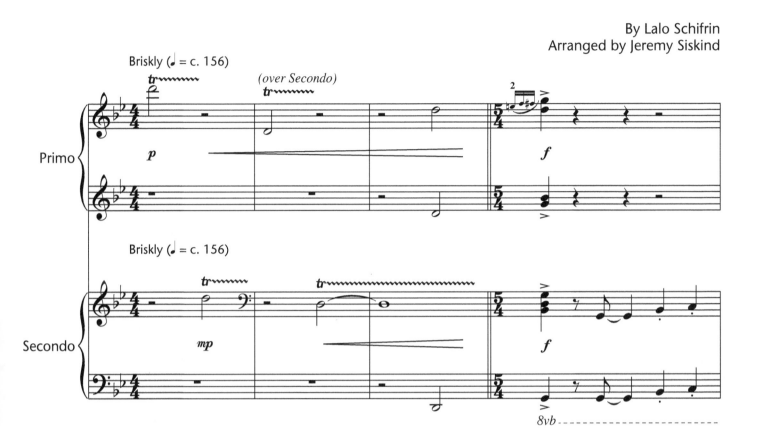

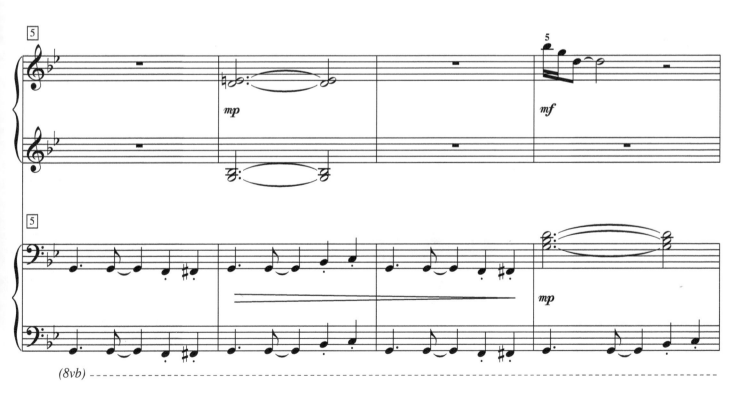

The Pink Panther

from THE PINK PANTHER

By Henry Mancini
Arranged by Jeremy Siskind

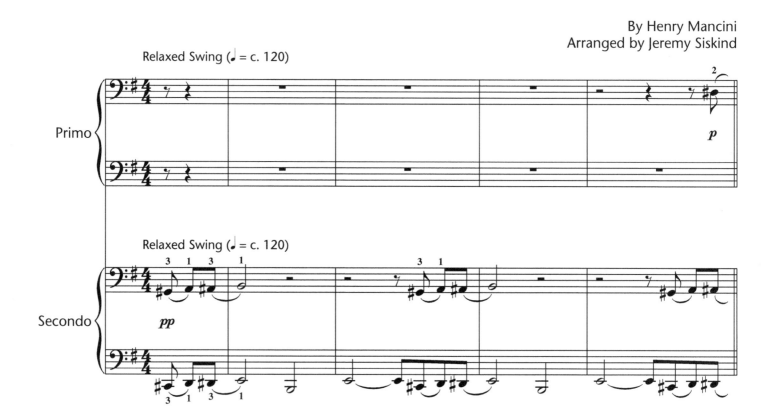

34

Secret Agent Man

from the Television Series

Words and Music by P.F. Sloan
and Steve Barri
Arranged by Jeremy Siskind

Soul Bossa Nova

Music by Quincy Jones
Arranged by Jeremy Siskind

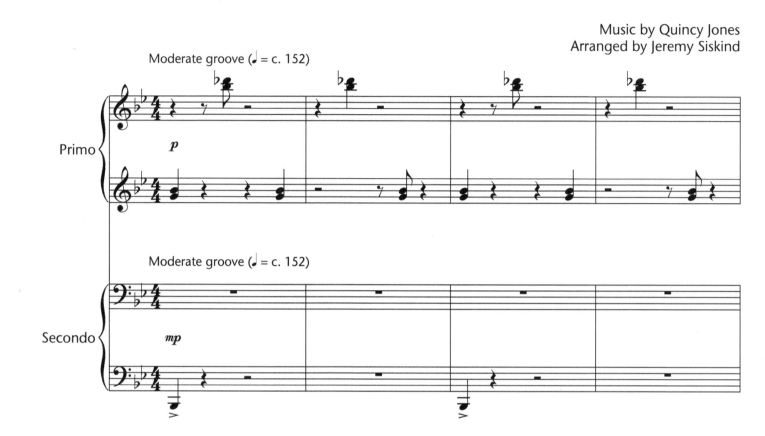